A Guide To Deception

By
Spencer Coffman

A Guide To Deception

While every precaution has been taken in the preparation of this book, the author and/or publisher assumes no responsibility for errors or omissions, or for damages resulting from the use of the information contained herein.

A Guide To Deception. Copyright © 2015 by Spencer Coffman. SpencerCoffman.com

Cover Design by Spencer Coffman

Photographs by Tom Webster

All rights reserved. Printed in the United States of America. This book may not be reproduced or transmitted, in whole or in part, in any form, or by any means, electronic or mechanical, including photocopying, recording, or by any information storage and retrieval system now known or hereafter invented, without written permission except in the case of brief quotations embodied in critical articles and reviews.

Library of Congress Cataloging-in-Publication Data

ISBN 978-0-9968562-0-1

Digital 978-0-9968562-1-8

Audio 978-1-9871536-3-7

• • •

A Guide To Deception

Dedication

This book is dedicated to you, the readers. May the content always be in your consciousness.

A Guide To Deception

Acknowledgments

First of all. Thank you, God, for giving me everything it took to write this book. The knowledge, the desire, the people who helped make it possible, the time to write it, the motivation and desire to complete the task, and the patience to see it through. I'm grateful to my family, immediate and extended. For without you I wouldn't be who I am today. Thank you, Scott, for writing such a great forward and for your willingness to do so. In addition, thank you for all of your assistance in reviewing this book. You've been a great help to me and I really appreciate it. Thank you. I would also like to thank Brad Strand for all of your guidance, motivation, and insight in the book publishing process. Without your advice, this book wouldn't have been possible. Thank you to Tom Webster for your desire to take the perfect cover photo, and for your patience in doing so. And thank you to you, the reader, for your desire to read this book. I sincerely hope you enjoy it.

> Thank you,
> Spencer Coffman

• • •

Acknowledgments

Are you tired of being lied to?

Imagine being able to know when someone was trying to pull the wool over your eyes. No longer will you be taken advantage of. You won't have to wonder anymore whether or not you are getting ripped off. Now you will simply know. You will be able to tell whether or not someone is lying or telling the truth just like that!

Do you wish you could tell, every time when someone was lying?

You see; body language is universal. That means it is the same on everyone. Therefore, when someone lies he or she displays the same signs as someone else. The good this is that…

These Signs Can Be Seen!

So, if you would like to be able to read people like Patrick Jane in The Mentalist and Cal Lightman in Lie To Me then **Keep Reading!**

It is possible for you to learn how to detect deception. With a little bit of practice you can learn how to read people and spot lies. You simply need to know what to look for.

That's why I've created this excellent book. It is dedicated to helping you learn about body language and the signs people display when they lie.

Introducing:

A Guide To Deception

You will learn:

* How to recognize lying eye contact
* What a shoulder shrug really means
* How someone feels when they cross their arms
* What it means when a person's voice changes
* That speech and body language must match
* And Much, Much, More…

A Guide To Deception is a short, and simple, six-chapter book that will teach you everything you need to know about detecting lies. You will learn how to read and interpret body language and emotional expressions that people display when they lie.

Acknowledgments

With the rising interest in psychology and human emotions, a great resource book such as this could easily be sold for $20 or more!

However, now you can get this excellent resource guide for a **special price!**

That's right. In addition, it's available on many online retailers and in a wide variety of formats. So you're sure to find one that works for you!

"Yes! I really want to discover how to read people and detect deception so that I can understand behavior and know when I'm being lied to before I get hurt.

So please send me my copy of "A Guide To Deception" - so I can start spotting lies and protect myself, starting today!

Claim Your Copy Today!

A Guide To Deception

Contents

S

Contents

Forward: By Scott Stumpf

Introduction: Why You Need This Book

How to Use This Book

Chapter One: Why The Truth Hurts

Chapter Two: Defining Deception

Chapter Three: Types of Lies

Chapter Four: The Ability to Detect Deception

Chapter Five: The Body's Betrayal

Chapter Six: Signs of Deception

Conclusion: What This Means For You

Appendix: List of Deceptive Behaviors

References

Index

§

Forward

By
Scott Stumpf

A Guide To Deception

Learning the art of knowing whether or not someone is deceiving you, or attempting to deceive you, is not only for law enforcement or those involved in national security. It is something for the everyday person as well. Don't fool yourself, deception occurs around everyone, not only those who have the stereotypical careers with deceit. Knowing when someone is lying is just as important for schoolteachers and parents as it is for law enforcement and government officials. No matter what you do, you are being lied to at some point. Whether they are little lies or big lies, many of us are lied to multiple times every day. Those lies might be coming from strangers, loved ones, or even co-workers. And trust me, if you have kids, you are definitely being lied to on some occasion or another. How often do you know you're being lied to? Some of the time, part of the time, none of the time? Wouldn't it be nice to know when this is happening to you? It'd sure make the conversations in life a lot more clear. When you hold this book you have the skills of a professional in your hands. All you have to do is study this information and you will be better at detecting deception. In addition, the information in this book will help you know exactly when someone might be lying to you.

My law enforcement career began in 1986, almost 30 years ago. I spent nine years as an investigator, and during those years I dealt with deception every day. Whether I was questioning a suspect in an interview room or a driver who said they didn't know they were speeding, I often knew I was being lied to. I almost

Forward

expected it. I guess working in one of those stereotypical careers of deceit can make that happen. Currently, I'm still working part-time as a cop. However, now I'm a law enforcement instructor at an accredited college. And let me tell you, deception is just as prevalent with students as it was with citizens. As I was reading this book, I thought about the many times I've been lied to as an instructor; "My homework isn't done because..." or "I was late for class because..." My job might have changed, but the fact that I was often being lied to didn't.

Spencer and I met in 2007 as youth leaders at our church. I was immediately drawn to his ability to communicate with people of all ages. Spencer effortlessly conversed with the other leaders who were more than twice his age! In addition, he was great with the kids and related to them as well as he was able to relate to the adults. Many young adults lack the ability to communicate, especially with older adults, but this seemed to be an area of strength for Spencer. We immediately became friends as I responded to his level of maturity and his leadership skills. He was well motivated, and I knew he wouldn't stand still in life; needless to say, he didn't disappoint. Spencer has obtained an impressive resume with over eight different certificates, degrees, and diplomas including Bachelor of Arts degrees in both Psychology and Philosophy as well as certificates in TESOL (Teaching English to Speakers of Other Languages) for both children and advanced learners. Spencer thrives on learning and excels in anything to which he is dedicated. If Spencer decides to do something it isn't a matter of whether or not it gets done. It's a matter of how many expectations he exceeds and how many jaws drop in the process. A simple example is, the time he completed a twelve to eighteen-month locksmithing diploma in only four months, all when he was fourteen years old! No matter the subject, Spencer dedicates himself with discipline and self-determination. He pours his passion for this craft of deception into a text for the layperson that isn't overwhelming and very easy to understand. He effortlessly points out that it is a skill that many of us will find useful in our everyday lives.

When Spencer first contacted me about writing this forward, my initial thought was, "Book? You're too young to write a book!" But when I realized that he'd already published a research article in an academic journal while he was in college, it occurred to me that he was no longer the young adult leader at our church. He'd grown up and was progressing. So, after publishing an article, it only makes sense that a book would come next. I told him I had never done anything like this before. I was uncertain and mentioned that forwards are generally written by well-known people or leaders in the subject matter, of which I am neither. Spencer didn't care. He wanted me to write his forward despite my telling him that I didn't believe I was qualified. Spencer reassured me, saying that he considered me to be both qualified and related to the field. After that, I told him that I was flattered by the request, but that I wouldn't be offended if he found someone more suited for the task. Still, Spencer persisted, insisting that I was going to write his forward.

Forward

My thought after that was, "Nobody reads the forward anyway and so what do I have to lose?" So I read his book and began writing. Now, after several months, many revisions, reading and re-reading it countless times, and two drafts for Spencer's comments the forward is written. It was a long process, but after having read the book, and seeing the enthusiasm Spencer has for this subject, I'm glad I agreed to do it and I feel very privileged to be writing a forward for such a gifted writer.

Throughout my career, in law enforcement and teaching, I've been to numerous schools on interviewing and how to detect deception. Even with my experience, I found this book to be both insightful and informative. It provides the necessary background information and valuable tools needed to help you detect deception. It's laid out in a quick-reference format that is user-friendly and easy to read. Spencer even adds a "how to" section at the beginning of the book, which is one of my favorite sections. It is so perfectly laid out and explained that I'm convinced anyone who can read would be able to read this book and gain the knowledge herein. Provided they follow the "how to" that is. Spencer helps the reader process the material by asking that the book first be read through in its entirety without stopping, and then again to help the reader retain what they have read. I found this method to be both helpful and unique, and the easy-read format makes it all possible.

The information in this book can serve most any person and make them better at detecting deception.

A Guide To Deception

It is a great book to read for the person who has no training in detecting deception or the person who is very knowledgeable in detecting deception. Whether you know nothing about detecting deceit or you know it all and are simply looking to hone your skills, this book is for you. It is a great book written by an ordinary person with a passion for emotions, facial expressions, and body language who simply wants to share his knowledge with the rest of us. If you would like to know when you are being deceived, definitely, read this book.

Scott Stumpf

• • •

Introduction:
Why You Need This Book

If you're already reading this book I don't need to tell you why you need it. You already know why you need it. You need this book because sometime in your life someone has lied to you. You need this book because you are involved in important relationships with your friends, family, coworkers, clients, et cetera. You need this book because you are someone who lives in the world of people instead of under a rock and you want to make sure that when you're buying a car, appliance, insurance, or some other item, that you aren't getting ripped off.

A Guide To Deception

Basically, you need this book because you want to be able to know whether or not the people you encounter are being honest with you.

Everyone needs this book.

• • •

How to Use This Book

This book is designed to be a short and simple read providing you with an overview knowledge of deception. Read each chapter thoroughly, and once you begin a chapter read it in its entirety. No pausing in the middle of a chapter! The only time you can stop reading is when you arrive at the end of a chapter. So make sure you allow plenty of time to read all the way through. Page ahead to see how long each chapter is and use your best judgment on how long it will take you to thoroughly read it. Read the entire book. Forget about pausing to highlight or underline anything. Don't worry about spending time visualizing any of the signs. Simply continue reading. This is your quick pass, the overview of the material.

Then, once you have finished the book. Go back and re-read it. The second time you may skim over parts you understand and slow down on parts that are confusing to you. Take the time to highlight, underline, and comment on the book. Write your own hints and tips in the margins. Make it yours. If you notice any bit of information that you want to know more about, or there is something you that don't fully understand, look at the reference number. Then turn to the References section and write down the source. Make the effort to look it up and read it. A simple search on the Internet should bring up the manuscript.

When you arrive at Chapter Six during your second reading make sure you are in a place where you are able to concentrate. This time attempt to visualize each of the different signs you read about. If you can't visualize them, then take the time to try them out yourself. Use a mirror if you have to. Do whatever you have to do to be able to mentally picture what the sign looks like in your head. In this way, you will be training your conscious mind to notice these unconscious behaviors.

After finishing Chapter Six, continue on through the rest of the book. Then, when you arrive at the Appendix, read the list and try to visualize each of the

How to Use This Book

signs once more. You may want to flip back and forth from the Appendix to Chapter Six so that you can read the paragraph description as well as the listed sign. Really dig in and make sure you understand the material. Then, continue reading and finish the book. From time to time, refer back to Chapter Six and the Appendix for reference and to keep these signs fresh in your conscious mind.

In essence, there are three simple steps to this book. Read it, re-read it, and study it. Like anything, practice makes perfect. The more you come back to this material and study it the more you will notice these behaviors in your everyday life. Basically, you get what you put into it. If you want to become a human lie detector then you need to make studying these signs a part of your everyday life. Stick with it, and within a few months of reviewing you'll be seeing signs all around you.

                              Best of luck!
                              Spencer Coffman

● ● ●

A Guide To Deception

A Guide To Deception

A Guide To Deception

Chapter One:
Why The Truth Hurts

She is heartbroken. Who knew information could be so devastating. For months she's suspected her husband of having an affair. However, it was simply too difficult to think about. Every time she began to examine the signs she would make herself stop. "I don't care" she would say, "I'm happy". She would reason with herself, remembering that it was a long process to find love again. Perhaps a cheating husband was better than no husband at all. At least she had somebody, even though he was only half there. Although the longer it went on the more she hurt. The feelings of not knowing, the uncertainty, it was unsettling. Then he told her.

He said he had found someone else. That he had been seeing her for a while and that they were moving in together. He would soon be leaving her for another woman and that was the truth. She had never felt so much pain. Suddenly it all seemed so real. Like it was no longer a fantasy in her head that she could explain away. All her speculation and accusations were true. She had known it all along but was too afraid to face the truth. Now she had no choice. The truth was staring her right in the face. And she had no choice but to accept it. This was her new reality, and it hurt.

Lies occur all around us, whether it is a little white lie or a more serious lie; it is something that people do every day.[1] In addition to lying, people also tell the truth, some do so right away and others lie first. However it comes out, the truth is a powerful thing that is capable of causing all kinds of problems, especially when followed by a lie. So why does the truth hurt? And why is it, that sometimes it is easier to lie than to tell the truth? Believe it or not, the answers are scientifically based. Since we are used to being lied to, and not accustomed to the truth, when it is finally revealed, it is so shocking that it can cause emotional strain. Another problem is that anytime someone receives information it is usually a combination of auditory and visual stimuli, which the human brain processes at different rates.[2] In addition, these stimuli are also processed in many different areas of the brain,[3]

Chapter One

at first together, in the inferior colliculus, and then it is separated and sent to the temporal or occipital lobe.[4] The amazing difference in the traveling speeds of auditory and visual information further complicates the issue.

The speed of sound is 1/5 of a mile per second,[5] which is significantly slower than the speed of light at 186,000 miles per second.[6] This difference is so drastic that it is hardly even comparable. Nonetheless, it is clear that visual stimuli reach the brain faster than auditory stimuli[7] because it travels at a much greater speed. In addition, visual stimuli are also much more complex than auditory stimuli.[8] Due to its complexity, and the fact that there is more visual than auditory stimuli, it is processed more slowly.[4] Another factor is that the louder the auditory stimuli, the more quickly it is processed. Thus creating even more of a discrepancy.[9]

In other words, visual stimuli reach the brain long before auditory stimuli. However, it takes much longer to process. Therefore, even though sound comes later it is processed faster because it is less complex. Sometimes this discrepancy can be observed, such as when you see something far away and then hear the sound. Or when you hear something and then see what is making the sound. Basically, in order for people to understand what they are seeing and hearing the brain is constantly shifting reality so that the world of lights and sounds synchronizes by the time the stimuli is processed. The brain is completing advanced computations so that we can understand what is going on in a matter of milliseconds. The brain is making up for the discrepancy between auditory and visual stimuli by deceiving us into believing that sound and light occur simultaneously. In other words, human's brains are constantly lying to them.

This is best demonstrated by the interpretation of ventriloquists and their puppets. To the observer, it appears as though the puppet's mouth and the sound of the ventriloquist's voice occur simultaneously. Due to the brain shifting reality to make up for the discrepancy of the auditory stimuli being processed faster than the visual stimuli, even though the visual stimuli reaches the brain before the auditory stimuli. This shift in reality creates the illusion that the sound is coming from the puppet's mouth, when, in fact, it is coming from the ventriloquist's.

The brain is lying to us so that we are able to understand what is happening. Without these lies, people would not know which sounds go with which sights or vice versa. There would be a constant chaos of lights and sounds each occurring at different rates that would be nearly impossible to decipher. Luckily, the brain does all of that for us so that by the time we consciously see and hear these lights and sounds we are able to understand them. To put it simply, lies are what make the world make sense. People understand lies, they are used to them. However, when the truth is revealed it doesn't make sense. It is something people are unaccustomed to and it is hard for them to understand. Thus, "the truth hurts".

• • •

Chapter Two:
Defining Deception

It was a typical day for the businessman. Today, like every day for the past five years, he drove to work and parked his car outside the office in the same spot. Today, however, would be different. At some point during the morning, an associate of his asked him if he wanted to go to lunch today. Of course, the businessman agreed and offered to drive. He told the associate that his car was parked right outside in its usual place. However, unbeknownst to the businessman, his car was stolen this morning. Not long after the businessman parked his car, someone decided to break in and drive it off. At lunchtime, the businessman and his associate walked out to the parking space and, to their surprise, found that there was no car as the businessman had said. Did the businessman lie to his associate? The answer to that question depends on the definition of deception.

Over the years, deception has been defined in several different ways with each definition possessing its own problems. Early on, the parameters that constituted a lie were very broad and unspecific. However, as time, and the study of deception progressed, new parameters were added to refine the definition of deception. Each consecutive definition became more and more specific and yet more and more broad, in that the spectrum of lies that it defined was increased. Of course there have been many different definitions proposed over the years, however, there have only been a few different widely accepted working definitions.

Krauss proposed one of the first major working definitions of deception in 1981.[1] He defined deception as:

'an act that is intended to foster in another person a belief or understanding which the deceiver considers to be false'.

Chapter Two

According to this definition, deception is an intentional act in which the deceiver is knowingly attempting to deceive another person. Thus, the businessman who told his associate that his car was parked outside only to find out it was stolen when they went to the parking space was not lying. The businessman thought his car was parked outside and thought that what he told his associate was indeed the truth. He discovered it was false at the same time as his associate when they both went to find the car. Therefore, since he was not knowingly attempting to deceive his associate the businessman was telling the truth according to this definition of deception.

In addition to verbally lying, this definition also covers nonverbal lies and silent actions. For example, the athlete who fakes a foot injury or takes a dive is engaging in deception by actively withholding information. The athlete is knowingly attempting to deceive others by performing at a level below normal. Only the athlete knows for certain that he or she is going to lose. Other people may speculate, however, the athlete knows and is, therefore, lying according to this definition of deception.

This seems to be a pretty good definition of deception. It covers verbal and nonverbal behaviors and even allows for those who have unknowingly lied. However, the parameters may be too narrow in that deception is restricted as an act that only occurs within humanity. When in reality animals, and even some plants, knowingly engage in deception. In 1986, Mitchell[2] came up with perhaps one of the most remarkable definitions of deception. He said that deception is:

> *'a false communication that tends to benefit the communicator'.*

This definition is very simple and easy to understand. It's broad enough to cover verbal and nonverbal communication and, of course, this definition implies that not only humans but also other living things, such as plants and animals, engage in acts of deception.

Bond and Robinson,[3] agree with this notion. They describe how the *ophrys speculum* tricks male wasps into pollinating them by presenting the illusion of sexual contact. The center of the orchid is colored so that it resembles a female wasp. Not only that, but the plant produces a scent that mimics insect sexual pheromones to attract and arouse male wasps. Once the male has arrived at the center of the flower, it finds long thick hairs that resemble a female wasp's abdomen. The male believes he has found a mate and pseudo-copulation occurs. The wasp then moves onto another orchid and is drawn in by the same mechanisms and the orchid is cross-pollinated in the process. The orchid is engaging in

Chapter Two

deception because it is lying to the male wasp, convincing the wasp that it has found a mate. The wasp mates with the plant and then moves on to another plant while believing that he is mating with a female wasp. This is a false communication in which the benefit is greater for the communicator.

Mitchell and Anderson[4] found that capuchin monkeys engage in deception by hiding food and misleading other monkeys in an effort to protect their own stash. These monkeys would find food and stash it for themselves. Then, they would mislead other monkeys away from their own stash. Thus, deceiving the other monkeys. DeWaal[5] gives some examples of more sophisticated animal deceit. He explains that male chimpanzees use bluffing displays to figure out which of the chimps is the strongest. Sometimes, when faced with a fearsome opponent, chimps will involuntary bare their teeth, which can undermine the chimp's bluff of strength. Most chimps are able to sense this involuntary baring of teeth and turn their back before it happens. They then resume their bluff once the expression is gone. In one instance, DeWaal observed that a chimp quickly used his fingers to push his lips back over his teeth so that his bluff of strength would continue.

Although Mitchell's definition included plants and animals, it failed to specify that deception is an intentional act, and therefore implies that unconsciously and mistakenly misleading others is classified as deception. Thus, according to Mitchell's definition, the businessman mentioned earlier would be lying to his associate. Most people don't believe that the businessman was lying since he himself didn't know he was lying. As a result, most people tend to agree with the definition introduced by Krauss in 1981. However, Krauss' definition ignores an aspect of deception that is bought up by Ekman in 1992.[6] He says that people are only lying when they fail to inform others, in advance, of their intention to lie. Thus, magicians aren't lying, because even though they are deliberately trying to deceive their audience, the audience is expecting to be deceived.

Ekman's definition of deception is as follows:

> 'a deliberate choice to mislead a target without giving any notification of the intent to do so'.

This definition is broad enough to include all aspects of the previous definitions and seems to be the best definition yet. According to this definition, the businessman would not be lying as he didn't intend to mislead his associate, the target. The athlete, orchid, monkey, and chimp would all be considered to be lying as they were deliberately misleading their targets. However, this definition isn't very specific in what it includes since without the knowledge of the previous definitions of deception one would assume that it applies

Chapter Two

to humans and would fail to think of plants and animals. Nevertheless, if it were brought up, this definition is clearly broad enough to include all species even though it is very brief and nonspecific.

Aldert Vrij[7] says that Ekman's definition is incomplete, but not because of its failure to mention plants and animals, but because it fails to include successful and unsuccessful attempts at lying. However, it would seem apparent that whether an attempt to deceive is successful or unsuccessful they are both lies. In one case the liar wasn't believed and in the other, the liar was believed and got away with the lie. Nonetheless, Vrij says that liars are sometimes unsuccessful in misleading their targets even though they have a clear intention to do so. In addition, sometimes the target may know that the liar is lying, and in this case, the act of deception is still considered a lie. Basically, Vrij emphasizes that unsuccessful attempts at lying are still considered lies. Whether they are found out, or simply not believed, they are still considered lies, even if only the liar knew about it.

He, therefore, defines deception as:

> '*a successful or unsuccessful deliberate attempt, without forewarning, to create in another a belief which the communicator considers to be untrue*'.

This definition has the simplicity of Ekman's definition and includes both successful and unsuccessful attempts at lying. In addition, it also specifies that the communicator knows the information is untrue, thus encompassing Krauss' definition. Therefore, like Ekman's definition, the businessman wouldn't be lying as he wasn't deliberately intending to mislead. However, athlete, orchid, monkey, and chimp would all be considered to be lying as they were deliberately misleading their targets. Vrij's definition is specific enough to define traits and broad enough to include all species and aspects of nature and is therefore perhaps the best single definition of deception among science today.

• • •

Chapter Three:
Types of Lies

    There are two types of lies, low-stake lies and high-stake lies.[1] Low-stake lies are the everyday white lie in which the liar's consequence is primarily embarrassment.[1] These are the so-called "polite" or "social" lies that are told in everyday conversation. Some examples include: I love your shirt, your cooking is great, I'm busy today, et cetera. Without these lies, conversations could become awkward and unnecessarily rude. Imagine a conversation where someone has cooked a meal for another person. In our current social world, the correct, polite, response would be a positive one no matter how the food really is. However, responding with a negative answer, even if it is the truth, isn't polite and is, therefore, an unacceptable response.

In addition, social interactions could become very unpleasant, and awkward, if people told the truth all of the time. Consider the outcome if every time you spoke with someone, your boss, for example, you told him or her how you really feel. Chances are a lot more people would be out looking for jobs. Humans like to be praised and they love to feel good about themselves. No one wants to hear how bad they look or how terrible their cooking is. Perhaps this is why people often enjoy the company of those who lie frequently.[2] Lies make people feel good, and many con artists have used this to their advantage. The fact is, that low-stake lies, white lies, are a part of everyday conversation. If people don't lie then they don't fit in very well with society and, as a result, aren't very popular. They are seen as rude, inconsiderate, or awkward.

On the other hand, high-stake lies are a much more serious matter in which the consequences could be detrimental to both the liar and the liar's target.[1] Involvement in a high-stake lie is risky business. The liar no longer risks embarrassment, but perhaps severe and extreme punishment, and/or emotional damage. High-stake lies are most commonly found in matters of national security, political campaigns, or having an affair. High-stake lies have a real purpose and the people

Chapter Three

who use them mean business. It is way beyond saving someone's embarrassment or preventing hurt feelings. High-stake lies can ruin lives. Spies are notorious for using high-stake lies and, if they are found out, it could cost them their life and the lives of others. Blackmail is another form of high-stake lie in which someone uses a high-stake lie to force someone else into a high-stake lie of their own. High-stake lies are very stressful and hard to keep up with. These are the kind of lies that wear people out. Where low-stake lies are fun and social, high-stake lies are draining and eventually lead to pure exhaustion mentally, physically, and emotionally. Of course, becoming a good liar doesn't happen overnight and takes years to master.

The ability to lie is a learned behavior that is most often taught by parents.[3] Children learn to lie through the examples of others. They don't realize what they are doing but are simply doing as they're told. In addition, most parents don't realize that what they are really teaching their children is how to become a better liar. For parents, they are simply teaching their children how to behave politely and not offend anyone. For example, how often does a parent tell their child to pretend to like the present they were given or the food presented to them at the table? It happens all of the time. Polite society and lying go hand in hand. Thanks to parents, and other role models, many children are skilled liars.[4] However, the ability to deceive tends to increase with age.[5] Thus, theoretically, the older a person is the better liar they are. Human lie detectors have a harder time detecting lies told by older children than younger children,[6] which supports the fact that people become better liars as they age. In addition, lie detectors have more difficulty detecting lies told by 79 year-olds than by 19 year-olds.[7] Like anything, practice makes perfect, and the older a person is the more practice he or she will have.

Lying may also be viewed as an act of self-preservation.[8] As a person ages, they have a lot more life history and a greater reputation to preserve. Each year a person ages they have another year of experiences that they are able to lie about. They can use these life experiences and knowledge to come up with more intricate, and more believable, lies. Continuing with this reasoning, as a person ages he or she would have more practice lying in an attempt to self-preserve and would thus become a better liar.[9]

The fact is, humans lie, and are lied to, every day.[3] The average person tells two to three lies in ten minutes of conversation,[10] so the more someone talks the more he or she is lying. In addition, people are lied to close to two-hundred times per day.[11] That means that if you get eight hours of sleep a night you are on the receiving end of about twelve lies an hour. Other research has shown that the average person tells anywhere from four to six lies per day.[12] Thus, the calculation claiming that each person is lied to around two-hundred times per day may vary depending on how many people one interacts with and how long the conversations last.

The bottom line is, lies are everywhere. If people

Chapter Three

aren't receiving them from other people they are giving them to other people. They are unavoidable and play a key role in today's world. In addition, human's brains are constantly lying to them as it shifts reality to synchronize the abundance of auditory and visual stimuli so that we can comprehend what is going on in the world around us. Therefore, it is vitally important to be able to recognize the signs of deception and be able to tell the difference between truth and falsity. In the case of a low-stake lie, it may save your feelings from being hurt. In the case of a high-stake lie, it may save your life.

• • •

A Guide To Deception

Chapter Four: The Ability to Detect Deception

Due to the fact that there are so many verbal and nonverbal cues to deception, it would seem that the general population would be able to accurately detect deceit. However, most of the research on deception doesn't state an argument for or against peoples' ability but reports specific research findings. The wizards project conducted by Paul Ekman and Maureen O'Sullivan, from 1990 to

2005, examined over 20,000 people from many different career areas, including businessmen, law enforcement workers, government workers, teachers, students, and many more. They found that when detecting deception people perform at or around a chance level of 50%.[1]

In addition, they identified only fifty people who possess the ability to accurately detect deception without any formal training.[2] These people were termed "wizards" due to their almost inhuman ability to read other peoples' emotions.[1] Accurately was defined as 70% or greater. Another study found that people in career areas that depend on the ability to detect deception have greater accuracy than those who don't. For example, 53% of the Secret Service agents tested achieved an accuracy rate of at least 70%, and 29% of the agents achieved an accuracy rate of at least 80%.[3] Even though these people were able to perform at a rate significantly above chance, they were not considered "wizards" because their ability was most likely due to their training and experience.

Ekman, O'Sullivan, and Frank[4] conducted a follow-up study that aimed to account for any discrepancies that could have made the Secret Service appear better than they were, as these were the only people, other than the fifty wizards, out of over 20,000 that were able to perform significantly higher than chance. They tested over 600 people involved in law enforcement and psychology careers. In an effort to make the truths and lies seem more real, they offered incentives to actors involved in making the stimuli. Truth tellers received a $10 bonus if they were believed, and liars received a $50 bonus if they were believed. They found that performance was better in judging lies than truths and that the majority of the participants performed at or below chance. They concluded that the Secret Service's superior ability was most likely due to their job training and experience indicating that if taught, people can detect deception.

In support of these claims, Porter, Juodis, ten Brinke, Klein, and Wilson[5] found that after receiving a three-hour training session on verbal and non-verbal behaviors participants' accuracy ratings improved from an average of 51% to 60%. Driskell[6] examined the relationship between training and the ability to detect deception when he conducted a meta-analysis of sixteen studies representing the behavior of 2,847 trainees. He concluded that, in general, the ability to detect deception increases after receiving training. Further, the type of training implemented, training content, trainee expertise, and the type of lie told, all affected accuracy ratings. Vrij[7] came to a similar conclusion after analyzing eleven studies in which participants received a brief training session and found that, with training, a person's ability to accurately detect deception increased by an average of 5% to 10%.

Conversely, Vrij notes that in three studies the training had adverse effects on the ability to detect deception and claimed that this was because the participants were police officers who most likely ignored the training and used their own "rules of thumb", learned in their job training, to detect deception. Similarly, Bull[8] reviewed several police training books and tutorials and found that most of the information appears to deceive the readers and, therefore, a training effect does not exist. Docan-Morgan[9] expresses the same concerns in his article, in which, he says that law enforcement officers are poor at detecting deception because they are receiving bad or incorrect training. In addition, they are following their "general principles" instead of science. In the end, he proposes a new model for training that he hopes will provide a conceptual framework for thinking about deception detection training in the future.

Paul Ekman has developed a training tool using his Facial Action Coding System (FACS) that can teach people how to recognize emotions by reading micro-expressions of the face.[10] Results indicate that in as little as an hour, someone can improve their emotion detecting skills by about 25%.[11] Thus, after one hour of training the entire population could detect deception and other emotions by reading micro-expressions at a level of accuracy equal to that of the wizards. In addition, Pamela Meyer[12] says that she studied micro-expressions using Ekman's system and is a better lie-spotter because of it.

A significant amount of the research seems to support the position that the average person cannot accurately detect deception. According to Navarro and Schafer[13] and Navarro and Karlins,[14] there are many behaviors, as mentioned before, that people display when they are being deceptive. However, these behaviors don't always occur when a person is lying. For instance, if someone is comfortable with lying they may not show signs of stress.[15]

Therefore, they say that it is very difficult, if not impossible for a person to be able to accurately detect deception without formal training. In addition, they claim that anyone who can accurately detect deception has had training and, therefore, knows when the behavior is indicative of deception, and when it means something else, such as someone being cold or happy. The results of the meta-analysis conducted by Bond and DePaulo[16] and the results of chance detection found during the wizards project serve to support these claims. In fact, Bond and DePaulo said that due to the fact that 53% accuracy rate is about the same as a guess people don't have the ability to detect deception.

Similarly, O'Sullivan[2] proposed that most people cannot accurately detect deception, but a few can. These select few, are the "wizards" mentioned before. In her article, she states that there are a vast number of verbal and nonverbal behaviors that are indicative of deception. However, the mere fact that there are many behaviors doesn't mean that they are noticed. In fact, most people do not consciously pay attention to the nonverbal behavior. Those that do, have either had formal training or possess a natural ability. More recent research has suggested that these human behaviors occur all of the time even when deception isn't present.[17] They stated that deceptive behaviors could only be considered deceptive when they appear with other deceptive behaviors. This is similar to the behavior cluster theory proposed by Nierenberg and Calero,[18] which stated that people must look for clusters of behaviors rather than individual behaviors.

Perhaps the main reason that people are unable to accurately detect deception is because they don't want to be able to detect other people's lies. It is also very likely that people don't want to know the truth.[19] As stated in Chapter One, the truth hurts. Thus, people may prefer to live in their ignorance, as ignorance is often bliss. In addition, most of the lies that people encounter are low-stake lies. Therefore, does it really matter if someone is able to detect them? For instance, if someone tells their friend that their new haircut looks good when, in reality, it is awful, the friend might be hurt if she were to be able to see the truth. Other instances might include giving someone a gift and not wanting to see the disappointment on their face when they don't like it.

In addition, people may not know what to do with the truth if they were to see it. Of course, this relates to whether or not someone wants to be able to know the truth in the first place. Nevertheless, consider the case of the wife who suspects her husband of having an affair. First of all, she may not want to know whether or not he is having an affair and second she may not know what to do if she confirms her suspicion. If she confronts her husband then he may be forced to make a choice between the two women. Rather than risking divorce she would

Chapter Four

rather live with a cheating husband than no husband at all. Until he leaves her, that is.

Yet another reason that people may not be able to detect deception is because the lie may not have been detectable. For instance, some people, such as pathological liars, those with antisocial personality disorder, and others, are very comfortable telling lies. Due to their comfort level, they most likely don't feel stressed and are therefore not likely to display many signs of leakage.[7] In addition, some liars tend to exhibit less bodily movements that truth tellers.[15]

Presumably, because they may be conscious of the truthfulness of their unconscious and wish to prevent it from showing.[7] Another difficulty is that there is no such thing as a typical deceptive behavior.[18] That is, liars may show any number of different behaviors or none at all.[14] In addition, the differences between liars and truth-tellers are very small so they may not even be noticed.[17] Thus, since people are not very good at noticing the verbal and non-verbal signs of leakage when they are present, they will most certainly overlook them if they are minimally present or not present at all.[2]

Finally, perhaps the biggest disadvantages in the ability to detect deception are the rules of conversation. After all, it is not polite, and you most likely won't be engaged in a conversation for very long, if you continually question each of your partner's statements in an attempt to notice their unconscious at work. In addition, while engaged in conversation, most people tend to look their partner in the eye, watch the area around the eyes, focus on the face, look around the room, et cetera. However, most of the telltale signs that form clusters of deceptive behavior are not present in any of these areas! It stands to follow that if someone is not paying attention to the hands, arms, legs, feet, torso, et cetera, then they will not be able to see any of the leakage emitted by these areas. After all, that which is not sought cannot be found.

    As this chapter has shown, the issue of whether or not people can accurately detect deception remains complicated. It would seem that an accuracy rate of 50% isn't very good, and therefore people aren't able to accurately detect deceit. However, the presence of "wizards" and the fact that people can receive formal training suggests that deception can be detected. If after one hour of training, with Ekman's training tool, people are able to increase their accuracy rating from 50% to 75% then this suggests that deception, or more specifically, micro-expressions can easily be detected. However, without the training, this detection ability wouldn't occur since the majority of people have no idea what constitutes a deceptive behavior or even where to look. Thus, at this point in time, it is safe to say that the average person is unable to detect deception since their accuracy rate is at or around a chance level. However, maybe in the future more people will receive formal training and will then be able to detect deception at a much higher rate.

● ● ●

Chapter Five:
The Body's Betrayal

With all of these lies occurring every day, how is it possible to know the truth and avoid becoming a victim of lies? The answer is relatively simple. Know when people are lying. In order to do this, one must be able to recognize what the body does when the mind is telling a lie. When people lie, the body produces unconscious verbal and non-verbal behaviors that are leaked by the person.[1] In other words, when people lie there are "tells" that the body displays without the person even knowing it. These behaviors occur because the unconscious is very truthful and non-deceptive.[2] It has only one moral rule and that is to tell the whole truth and nothing but the truth. As a result, when someone consciously tells a lie, their unconscious is constantly betraying them by producing truthful verbal slips and truthful non-verbal behavior.[3] A person may literally be saying one thing and doing another. The disagreement between the conscious lie and the unconscious truth results in a contradiction between normal speech and body language.[4] Sometimes it is very noticeable, and often times its hardly noticeable at all.

    If noticed, these behaviors can be interpreted and used to deduce the possibility of deception.[5] This is a very difficult task as not only must the leakage be noticed, but it must also be understood by the observer. Once it is understood then it can be used to determine whether or not the person was telling a lie. However, extreme caution must be undertaken, as these behaviors are vast in number and often differ depending on the person and the situation.[6] For instance, if someone crosses their arms, it does not always mean that they are being defensive or hiding something,[6] it could simply mean that they are cold, tired, or even bored.[5] For this reason, it is essential that if a person has the desire to become a human lie detector, he or she must learn to examine clusters, or patterns, of behavior rather than specific and individual behaviors.[3] It is a cluster of several individual behaviors that determine whether or not a person is lying,[3] and it is very rare for a liar only to exhibit one form of truthful verbal or non-verbal behavior.[3] The reason is that throughout the course of the entire lie, the unconscious is constantly producing truthful leakage.[1] These clusters of behavior can be interpreted and used to determine whether or not a person is lying. However, the difficult part is determining whether a certain behavior can be classified as part of a cluster, or if it is simply occurring because a person is cold, for example. This is a task that requires countless hours of studying and practice. Thus, it is vital to know where to look.

Liars attempt to disguise their facial expressions more than their bodily expressions when telling a lie.[7] This is most likely because, when speaking with others, the majority of people look at the face and not the other areas of the body. After all, how many times have you heard that it is important to maintain eye contact when speaking with someone? Children are taught it on a daily basis. Because liars attempt to disguise the face more than the body, their body is a better source of leakage than the face.[8] There are also more opportunities for nonverbal behaviors to leak from the body than the face.[9] This makes sense because the body is a larger area than the face, so of course there would be more sources of leakage. In addition, it is possible for someone to be silent verbally, by not speaking, in an effort to reduce the unconscious slips of the tongue or verbal leakage that may occur. However, it is impossible for him or her to be silent non-verbally.[10] No matter how hard they try their body is still going to move. Sooner or later they are going to have to breathe, blink, swallow, et cetera.

A Guide To Deception

Regardless of whether they are lying or telling the truth, the body will continue to leak truthful non-verbal behaviors.[11] The unconscious simply cannot help it. When someone is lying, the behaviors will contradict their statements and be more noticeable. When someone is telling the truth the behaviors will support their statements and be a natural part of their conversation. These unconscious nonverbal behaviors can occur all over the body.[12] However, they are mainly found in the eyes, head and neck, mouth, arms, hands, feet and legs, and in breathing and speech patterns.[5] Remember these areas, as the majority of truthful non-verbal leakage occurs there.[6] In addition to knowing the areas, it is also important to know the different signs of deception in each area. However, before these signs are explained it is necessary to mention the primary tool used for detecting deception among the face.

In an effort to make learning and discussing the structures in the face easier, Ekman and Friesen abandoned their Facial Affect Scoring Technique FAST[13] and decided to use the Facial Action Coding System FACS,[14] invented in 1978, to evaluate and assess universal facial expressions in emotions. They did so by photographing and recording the facial muscles and noting how they could be manipulated during the different states of emotion. Ekman and Friesen categorized all of the facial nerves and muscles into 44 Action Units (AU) in the FACS. Any facial movement can be described in terms of the particular action unit, or units, that it activates. For example, the zygomaticus major muscle

Chapter Five

(musculus zygomaticus major) is coded as AU12 and the orbicularis oculi (pars orbitalis) is coded as AU6. Thus, an enjoyment smile is coded as AU12+AU6. There is one more action unit that goes into an enjoyment smile and that is the separation of the lips (AU25, depressor labii inferioris). However, due to the fact that this action is also present in non-enjoyment smiles, it is not considered to be a distinguishing feature of smiling.[15]

The Facial Action Coding System is an important tool in the field of science. However, for everyday lie detection and for those who desire to become human lie detectors it is something that can be forgone until later on. The reason is, again, that most people attempt to disguise the face more than the body.[7] Therefore, anyone who wishes to be able to detect lies should focus on the body and learn to recognize the nonverbal leakage it displays. Then, once body language is understood, one can move on to understanding each of the different action units of the face and their meaning. Understand and remember this information, as it is the basis of knowing the different signs of deception within each leakage area, and the key to recognizing the different clusters of behavior, an action that may save your life or at the very least, your feelings.

• • •

A Guide To Deception

Chapter Six:
Signs of Deception

This is by no means a comprehensive list of all of the different signs of deception. However, it is a very good one in which many of the different signs are explained. Take the time to study and learn them and remember to look for clusters and patterns of behavior. If someone is lying there WILL be several different signs of deception. The unconscious simply can't help it, as long as the conscious is lying the unconscious will be telling the truth. The tough part is that it is unconscious. Learn to make these signs a part of your conscious. Recognize them so that when you observe them on other people they register in your conscious. Do this and, in no time at all, you'll be a human lie detector.

The different signs will be explained based on the different areas of the body. The eyes, the head and neck, the mouth, the hands and arms, the feet and legs, breathing, speech, and emotional expressions. As you read about each sign, take the time to visualize what it would look like on another person. In addition, try to act the sign out on yourself. This way you will be certain to know what it looks like and what it feels like when you do it. In doing this, you will be more self-aware the next time you unconsciously exhibit one of these signs.

The Eyes

Beginning with the eyes, researchers have shown that when people lie they increase eye contact,[1] supposedly to make sure their target believes the lie.[2] In addition, when people hear or see something that they disagree with, they may close their eyelids longer than a normal blink or flutter them rapidly.[3] They may also squint as if to shut out the unlikable stimuli.[2] A hand or finger movement to the eye usually follows this action in an unconscious attempt to block out the unlikable stimuli.[4] These hand and finger movements can occur without eye blinks as in when someone pretends to have something in their eye.[5]

The Head and Neck

Chapter Six

The head and neck are perhaps the most telltale signs of liars.[6] This could be why people try to mask their face more than their body when they tell lies.[7] The most frequent behavior is a person's head nodding "yes" while they are saying something like "I did not do it".[8] Other positive or negative verbal statements accompanied by the opposing non-verbal body language may also occur.[1] Saying yes while nodding no, saying no while nodding yes, or some other verbal to non-verbal contradiction. Truthful people tend to mirror head movements of the person with whom they converse, whereas a liar takes a more statuesque pose.[9] In addition, the muscles of the neck may tense up and the veins may protrude when someone is under pressure or duress.[4]

The Mouth

The mouth is another very telling feature.[3] When people lie their lips tend to take on all sorts of different positions.[8] People may bite their lower lip showing their two front teeth,[5] purse their lips as if they are sucking them inward making them disappear,[1] pucker their lips,[7] and frequently lick their lips.[4] In addition, when a lie is told, the corners of most peoples' lips tend to point downward for a split second.[10] Liars may also yawn repeatedly as if to convey boredom or relaxation.[9]

The Hands and Arms

Hand and arm movements are other behaviors

that can be useful in spotting liars.[1] Perhaps the most obvious behavior is when a liar curls up in an effort to take up as little space as possible.[11] He or she may back up into a corner, crouch down in a seated position, or curl up into a ball. This is unconsciously done to prevent others from seeing all of the other nonverbal behaviors that may give away their lie.[9] Liars may also touch the bottom of their nose with one finger, usually the index, in a side to side motion,[11] or place their hand on the back of their neck as if to massage away the tension.[12] They may also place their hand or fingers over their lips in a hushing position as if they are telling themselves to "shh".[8]

In addition, when a person crosses their arms,[11] reaches one arm across the chest to the opposite shoulder, or touches the neck dimple it may indicate that they are being defensive, withholding, or deceptive.[4] Similarly, when people, usually women, play with their necklace or men adjust their tie, they are usually under stress.[4] Another similar behavior that is indicative of lying is when a person gives a slight shoulder shrug when answering a question.[8] This is typically done with one shoulder more than the other and is not symmetrical like a normal shoulder shrug.[9] Often, people under stress or tension will wring their hands or tightly clasp them together.[1] They may also massage the fleshy part of the hand beneath the thumb with the thumb and index finger of the opposite hand.[2] In addition, behaviors such as nail biting, cuticle picking, or other hand grooming gestures may appear.[4]

Chapter Six

The Feet and Legs

A person's feet and legs may also give away their lie if they are not careful, as legs may be the best indicator of nonverbal behavior.[4] When a liar is accused of something and attempts to deny it, he or she will often take a step backward,[7] and sometimes raise their hands as if to ward off the accusation.[11] Some people may cross the bottoms of their legs at the calf muscle in an "X" like position as if to block the target's perceptions.[8] Others may lock the ankles together and tuck their feet back under the chair,[4] combining the "X" with backing away. They may also rapidly bounce both of their legs in a non-rhythmic fashion.[1] Although this is sometimes done in excitement, it is most likely done to release the stress or tension involved in telling a lie.[4] As with anything, the context of the situation is important.[9] After all, some people simply bounce their leg all of the time.

Occasionally, a liar may point him or herself towards the exit as if they are planning to escape from the situation.[2] Some people tend to pick up their legs and sit with them on the chair when they are being deceptive.[4] They will often place their heels on the edge of the seat with their knees right under their chin.[8] This is very similar to the example mentioned earlier of taking up the least amount of space possible, as confident people tend to spread out and dominate the space that they occupy.[2]

A Guide to Deception

Breathing

A person's breathing is also an indicator of deception,[4] as people who attempt to conceal information often breath more rapidly taking a series of shallow breaths followed by a longer deep breath after they have told the lie.[1] In addition, when a person is hiding something that the target is close to finding out, the liar will often hold their breath as the target guesses the possible answers.[11] On more occasions than not, the liar will exhale the instant the target guesses correctly.[2] Other instances involving breathing, that are indicative of tension or stress, include puffing up the cheeks then exhaling slowly through pursed lips,[10] breathing in through the nose and out through extended lips like those of a chimpanzee,[4] breathing regularly and periodically taking a deep breath followed by a long slow exhale,[2] and inhaling regularly and forcing the exhale as if the lungs are being forcibly contracted.[13]

Speech

Verbal cues are one of the most difficult to interpret when a person is lying,[13] mainly because there are many different ways in which a person's vocal inflections may change, and in how their sentences are formed.[14] The main thing to note is that liars prefer to conceal the truth rather than coming up with an entirely new story.[1] The main reason for this is because it is easier to remember something if part of it is true rather than to remember an entirely fictitious story.[4] When telling this story, a liar's mouth usually becomes very dry causing their voice to crack and stutter,[15] often times their Adam's apple may jump,[1] or their jaw may tremble[16] and, as mentioned before, liars may frequently lick their lips.[4]

Some people often say their statements twice with their voice rising the second time around.[2] They may also hesitate or use stalling tactics such as asking for the question to be repeated or rephrased.[17] In some cases, they may also rephrase the question and then answer it.[2] This is done to give them more time to think about their lie.[2] Another, more noticeable behavior, is that guilty people often avoid using contractions as if to emphasize their innocence.[11] For example, saying, "It was not me" instead of "It wasn't me".[2] Some liars may even make positive statements negative to provide quick answers to the question.[8] For instance, the question "did you cheat on your wife?" may be answered, "No, I did not cheat on my wife." A variation of this may occur when a person answered "yes" or "no" right away and the explanation comes more slowly as if they are thinking about what to say.[5]

However, perhaps the best way to detect a liar using their vocalizations is to say nothing.[2] Silence makes most people uncomfortable. When a person is telling a lie, they are under an immense amount of tension and stress,[4] thus they are already uncomfortable. When the target becomes silent, the liar's comfort level goes from bad to worse. Most of the time, the liar will continue to speak to fill the gap.[2] They will often continue to speak until they have convinced themselves that the target believes their story.[11] Other times, they may trip over their tongue and contradict themselves, thus revealing the truth.[5]

Emotional Expression

As far as emotional expression is concerned, one of the most telltale signs that a person is being deceptive is whether or not their facial expressions are symmetrical.[3] When people lie, they conjure up false emotions and behaviors in an attempt to make their lie more believable.[11] Symmetrical expressions are associated with telling the truth, as they are usually indicative of spontaneous emotional expressions.[18] They appear quickly without any conscious effort and are very fluid from start to finish.[18] Conversely, asymmetrical facial expressions are associated with deception and are usually indicative of non-spontaneous, or voluntary, emotional expression.[19] These expressions appear at a faster rate than spontaneous expressions and are much less fluid in their movements.[20]

Spontaneous emotional expressions are much more symmetrical than non-spontaneous emotional expressions with this asymmetry more prominently displayed on the left side of the face compared to the right.[21] This suggests greater involvement of the right cerebral hemisphere in false emotions or lies.[22] When adults portray enjoyment smiles (genuine enjoyment, truth) there is slightly greater activity in the left parietal

Chapter Six

lobe than any other lobe of the brain.[23] Conversely, when participants portrayed non-enjoyment smiles (fake enjoyment, lie) there was significantly greater activity in the right anterior temporal and parietal lobes.[23]

In general, the functions of each hemisphere of the brain are contra-laterally related to the body.[23] In other words, the right side of the brain controls the left side of the body and the left side of the brain controls the right side of the body. Non-spontaneous expressions are associated with the right cerebral hemisphere.[21] This explains why they are asymmetrical on the left side of the face. Spontaneous expressions activate the left cerebral hemisphere,[24] thus moving the right side of the face and equalizing the facial muscles used in facial expression.[25] This produces a symmetrical and more believable facial expression.[23] Thus, in general, if a person's expressions are symmetrical they are most likely telling the truth. However, if their expressions are asymmetrical there is a good chance they being deceptive.

Remember that this is not an all-inclusive list of all the potential signs of deception. In addition, people telling the truth may exhibit many of these signs. This is why it is essential to look for clusters or patterns of behavior. If you see one sign, note it, but don't immediately count it as a mark of deception. However, if you begin to see several signs, then consider the possibility that they are being deceptive. Learn to recognize these signs. Remember them, and begin to watch for them to occur when speaking with other people. The best way to start learning these signs is when you are not a part of the conversation. Observe others, that way you can be entirely focused on their body language and facial expressions. If you're in the conversation then you'll be focused on the verbal discussion rather than on the non-verbal language. Keep in mind that even though there are many signs of deception some people argue that detecting deception is simply guesswork. Prove them wrong and use what you have learned in this book to detect deception wherever it may occur.

• • •

Conclusion:
What This Means For You

Now that you have read this book you have a knowledge and understanding of unconscious nonverbal behavior that is unknown to most people. This knowledge can be unsettling at first, in that you may begin to feel transparent, like everything you do is being watched and is on display for the world to see. Remember, that this knowledge was unknown to you once before and it is most likely unknown to those around you. Therefore, don't worry, relax, and practice. Use your newfound knowledge to take your time and enjoy the self-consciousness that it produces in you. Pay attention to how you act, how others act, and always continue learning.

Take the time to read some of the books and articles mentioned in the References section. I strongly encourage you to do so. As mentioned several times before, this book is simply a quick study of nonverbal behavior, specifically deception. There are many more signs out there that weren't even mentioned in this book as well as other behavioral tendencies and patterns. In addition, there are behavior clusters for all kinds of emotions. By expanding your research you will be able to learn not only when someone is being deceptive, but also if they are sad, ashamed, angry, uncomfortable, nervous, et cetera. The more you learn the more you will realize you don't understand. Keep learning.

Use the list in the Appendix. Refer back to it time and time again and remember that it is simply a list. The behaviors and meanings are not set in stone. Periodically re-read Chapter Six and really practice and visualize the signs described there. You must always look for clusters and patterns of behavior. Simply because someone crosses their arms doesn't mean they are being defensive. However, if someone crosses their arms, steps backward, frowns, and shakes their head then they are most definitely being defensive.

Use what you have learned in this book to enhance your interactions with others. When you suspect someone is stressed or is being deceptive steer the conversation in a new direction. Then strategically

Conclusion

reintroduce the topic to confirm your suspicions. Use your knowledge to better yourself and those around you. If you simply call people out you'll only accomplish looking like a fool. You'll embarrass the liar and you'll gain a reputation for being an insensitive jerk. Before you ever call someone out in a lie ask yourself, does the truth really matter in that instance. Often times it will be trivial detail that those around you don't really care about or won't remember. They will remember your interruption though. Of course, you can always confront the liar privately if you wish to unsettle him or her.

The bottom line is, that if this is the only time you are going to read this book then you aren't going get much out of it. Learning to read people is like anything else. The more you practice the better you'll become. Read this book, re-read it, write in it, and refer back to it again and again. Make it a game. Say to yourself, today I'm going to focus on facial expressions or today I'm going to look for behaviors with the hands and arms. Keep practicing and never give up. When you are wrong, remember it and correct it. Engrave body language into your vocabulary and make it a part of your everyday life. Before long you'll be reading people like never before.

● ● ●

A Guide To Deception

§

Appendix:
List of Deceptive Behaviors

This is an itemized list of all the deceptive behaviors mentioned in this book. Keep in mind that there are many more deceptive behaviors and emotional expressions. This is by no means a comprehensive list. However, it is a very good one. Use this list as a quick reference guide after you have read about the different signs in Chapter Six. Remember that the meaning isn't set in stone. Simply because "increased eye contact" says "Lying" doesn't mean that it is always a lying behavior. Take the time to study and learn these signs and ALWAYS remember to look for clusters and patterns of behavior.

The signs are listed in order of their appearance in Chapter Six. Therefore, if you come across one that you don't understand, or can't visualize in your mind, turn back to the section in which it is explained. You must be able to visualize each of these signs in order to recognize them. Spend time practicing these signs; use a mirror so you will be able to see them on yourself. In doing this, you will be making these signs a part of your conscious behavior. Then, when they occur, you will be able to recognize them much more quickly.

The Eyes

Increased eye contact	Lying
Closing eyes longer than a normal blink	Disagreement
Rapidly flutter eyelids	Disagreement
Squinting	Block unlikable stimuli
Hands to the eye	Block unlikable stimuli

The Head & Neck

Appendix

Verbal/Non-verbal contradiction	Self-mistrust
Statuesque posing (not mirroring)	Withholding/Lying
Tense neck/protruding veins	Under pressure or duress

The Mouth

Bite lower lip displaying front teeth	Lying
Purse lips	Lying
Pucker lips	Lying
Frequently lick lips	Lying
Corners downward	Lying
Yawn repeatedly	Lying
Dry mouth	Lying

The Hands & Arms

Curling up	Lying
Touch bottom of nose	Lying
Touch back of neck	Lying
Hushing (fingers over lips)	Withholding

A Guide to Deception

Crossing arms	Defensive/Withholding
Arm to shoulder	Defensive/Withholding
Hand to neck dimple	Defensive/Withholding
Play with necklace	Stress
Adjust tie	Stress
Asymmetrical shoulder shrug	Lying
Wringing hands	Stress/Tension
Clasping hands	Stress/Tension
Massage hands	Stress/Tension
Grooming gestures	Stress/Tension

The Feet & Legs

Step backward (hands up)	Lying
Cross bottom of legs	Blocking
Locking ankles	Deceptive/Blocking
Rapidly bounce legs	Tension Release/Lying
Point towards exit	Escape
Sit with legs on chair	Withholding

Appendix

Breathing

Rapid breathing	Extreme Stress/Tension
Shallow breath deep breath	Lying
Holding breath	Withholding
Puffing cheeks	Stress/Tension
Chimpanzee lips	Stress/Tension
Regular breath long breath	Stress/Tension
Forced exhale	Stress/Tension

Speech

Voice crack	Lying
Stuttering	Lying
Jumping Adam's apple	Lying
Trembling jaw	Lying/Fear
Rising voice	Lying
Stalling tactics	Lying
Request question repeated	Lying
Rephrase then answer question	Lying
Avoiding contractions	Lying
Positive statements negative	Lying

A Guide To Deception

Instant answer followed by explanation	Lying
Continued talking	Lying
Contradicting themselves	Lying

References

Chapter One: Why The Truth Hurts

1 Ekman, P., & O'Sullivan, M. (1991). Who can catch a liar?. American Psychologist, 46(9), 913-920. doi: 10.1037/0003-066X.46.9.913

2 Binder, J., Frost, J., Hammeke, T., Bellgowan, P., Springer, J., Kaufman, J., & Possing, E. (2000). Human temporal lobe activation by speech and nonspeech sounds. Cerebral Cortex, 10(5), 512-528. doi: 10.1093/cercor/10.5.512

3 Perez, C., Engineer, C., Jakkamsetti, V., Carraway, R., Perry, M., & Kilgard, M. (2012). Different timescales

for the neural coding of consonant and vowel sounds. Cerebral Cortex, doi: 10.1093/cercor/bhs045

4 Groh, J., Trause, A., Underhill, A., Clark, K., & Inati, S. (2001). Eye position influences auditory responses in primate inferior colliculus. Neuron, 29, 509-518. 10.1016/S0896-6273(01)00222-7

5 NASA. (2010, September). Speed of sound. Retrieved from http://www.grc.nasa.gov/WWW/k-12/airplane/sound.html

6 NASA. (n.d.). how "fast" is the speed of light? . Retrieved from http://www.grc.nasa.gov/WWW/k-12/Numbers/Math/Mathematical_Thinking/how_fast_is_the_speed.htm

7 Thorpe, S., Fize, D., & Marlot, C. (1996). Speed of processing in the human visual system. Nature, 381, 520-522. doi: 10.1038/381520a0

8 Nettelbeck, T., & Wilson, C. (1985). A cross-sequential analysis of developmental differences in speed of visual information processing. Journal of Experimental Child Psychology, 40, 1-22. doi: 10.1016/0022-0965(85)90063-3

9 Polley, D., Heiser, M., Blake, D., Schreiner, C., & Merzenich, M. (2004). Associative learning shapes the neural code for stimulus magnitude in primary auditory cortex. Proceedings of the National Academy of Sciences, 101(46), 16351-16356. doi: 10.1073/pnas.0407586101

Chapter Two: Defining Deception

1 Krauss, R. (1981). Impression formation, impression

References

management, and nonverbal behaviors. In E. Higgins, C. Herman & M. Zanna (Eds.), Social cognition: The ontairo symposium (Vol. 1, pp. 323-341). Hillsdale, NJ: Earlbaum.

2 Mitchell, R. (1986). A framework for discussing deception. In R. Mitchell & N. Thompson (Eds.), Deception: Perspectives on human and nonhuman deceit (pp. 3-40). Albany, NY: State University of Ney York Press.

3 Bond, C., & Robinson, M. (1988). The evolution of deception. Journal of Nonverbal Behavior, 12, 295-307. doi: 10.1007/BF00987597

4 Mitchell, R., & Anderson, J. (1997). Pointing, withholding information, and deception in capuchin monkeys (cebus apella). Journal of Comparative Psychology, 111(4), 351-361. doi: 10.1037//0735-7036.111.4.351

5 DeWaal, F. (1986). Deception in the natural communication of chimpanzees. In R. Mitchell & N. Thompson (Eds.), Deception: Perspectives on human and nonhuman deceit (pp. 221-244). Albany, NY: State University of New York Press.

6 Ekman, P. (1992). An argument for basic emotions. Cognition and Emotion, 6(3), 169-200. doi: 10.1080/02699939208411068

7 Vrij, A. (2000). Detecting lies and deceit. West Sussex, England: John Wiley & Sons.

Chapter Three: Types Of Lies

1 Ekman, P., & O'Sullivan, M. (1991). Who can catch

a liar?. American Psychologist, 46(9), 913-920. doi: 10.1037/0003-066X.46.9.913

2 Vrij, A. (2000). Detecting lies and deceit. West Sussex, England: John Wiley & Sons.

3 Ekman, P. (2009). Telling lies. New York, NY: W. W. Norton.

4 Talwar, V., Crossman, A., Williams, S., & Muir, S. (2011). Adult detection of children's selfish and polite lies: Experience matters. Journal of Applied Social Psychology, 41(12), 2837–2857. doi: 10.1111/j.1559-1816.2011.00861.x

5 Edelstein, R., Luten, T., Ekman, P., & Goodman, G. (2006). Detecting lies in children and adults. Law and Human Behavior, 30, 1-10. doi: 10.1007/s10979-006-9031-2

6 Feldman, R., Jenkins, L., & Popoola, O. (1979). Detection of deception in adults and children via facial expressions. Child Development, 50, 350-355. doi: 10.2307/1129409

7 Parham, I., Feldman, R., Oster, G., & Popoola, O. (1981). International differences in nonverbal disclosure of deception. Journal of Social Psychology, 30, 261-269.

8 DePaulo, B. (1991). Nonverbal behavior and self-preservation: A developmental perspective. In R. Feldman & B. Rime (Eds.), Fundamentals of Nonverbal Behavior (pp. 351-379). New York, NY: Cambridge University Press.

9 Walters, S. (2000). The truth about lying. Naperville, IL: Sourcebooks.

10 Feldman, R., Forrest, J., & Happ, B. (2002). Self-presentation and verbal deception: Do self-presenters lie

References

more?. Journal of Basic and Applied Social Psychology, 24(2), 163-170. doi: 10.1207/153248302753674848

11 Meyer, P. (2010). Liespotting. New York, NY: St. Martin's Press.

12 Hartley, G., & Karinch, M. (2005). How to spot a liar. Pompton Plains, NJ: The Career Press.

Chapter Four: The Ability to Detect Deception

1 O'Sullivan, M., & Ekman, P. (2004). The wizards of deception detection. In P. Granhag & L. Stromwell (Eds.), The Detection of Deception in Forensic Contexts (pp. 764-780). Cambridge: Cambridge University Press. doi: 10.1017/CBO9780511490071.012

2 O'Sullivan, M. (2005). Emotional intelligence and deception detection: Why most people can't "read" others, but a few can. In R. Riggio & R. Feldman (Eds.), Applications of Nonverbal Communication (pp. 215-254). Retrieved from http://www.scribd.com/doc/20884972/Applications-of-Nonverbal-Communication-Ronald-E-Riggio

3 Ekman, P., & O'Sullivan, M. (1991). Who can catch a liar?. American Psychologist, 46(9), 913-920. doi: 10.1037/0003-066X.46.9.913

4 Ekman, P., O'Sullivan, M., & Frank, M. (1999). A few can catch a liar. Psychological Science, 10(3), 263-266. doi: 10.1111/1467-9280.00147

5 Porter, S., Juodis, M., ten Brinke, L., Klein, R., & Wilson, K. (2010). Evaluation of the effectiveness of a brief deception detection training program. The Journal

of Forensic Psychiatry & Psychology, 21(1), 66-76. doi: 10.1080/14789940903174246

6 Driskell, J. (2012). Effectiveness of deception detection training: A meta-analysis. Psychology, Crime & Law, 18(8), 713-731. doi: 10.1080/1068316X.2010.535820

7 Vrij, A. (2000). Detecting lies and deceit. West Sussex, England: John Wiley & Sons.

8 Bull, R. (1989). Can training enhance the detection of deception?. In J. Yuille (Ed.), Credibility Assessment (pp. 83-97). Dordrecht, The Netherlands: Kluwer Academic Publishers. doi: 10.1007/978-94-015-7856-1_5

9 Docan-Morgan, T. (2007). Training law enforcement officers to detect deception: A critique of previous research and framework for the future. Applied Psychology in Criminal Justice, 3(2), 143-171.

10 Ekman, P. (2008). Emotions revealed, recognizing faces and feelings to improve communication and emotional life. New York, NY: Owl Books.

11 Ekman, P. (2009). Telling lies. New York, NY: W. W. Norton.

12 Meyer, P. (2010). Liespotting. New York, NY: St. Martin's Press.

13 Navarro, J., & Schafer, J. (2001). Detecting deception. FBI Law Enforcement Bulletin, 9-12.

14 Navarro, J., & Karlins, M. (2008). What every body is saying, an ex-fbi agent\'s guide to speed reading people. (1st ed.). New York, NY: Harper Paperbacks.

15 Hartley, G., & Karinch, M. (2005). How to spot a liar. Pompton Plains, NJ: The Career Press.

16 Bond, C. J., & DePaulo, B. (2006). Accuracy of

References

deception judgments. Personality and Social Psychology Review, 10, 214-234.
17 Frank, M., Menasco, M., & O'Sullivan, M. (2008). Human behavior and deception detection. In J. Voeller (Ed.), Handbook of Science and Technology for Homeland Security (pp. 1-13). John Wiley & Sons, Inc. doi: 10.1002/9780470087923.hhs299
18 Nierenberg, G., & Calero, H. (1971). How to read a person like a book. New York, NY: Pocket Books.
19 Ekman, P. (1996). Why don't we catch liars?. Social Research, 63(3), 801-817

Chapter Five: The Body's Betrayal

1 Navarro, J., & Karlins, M. (2008). What every body is saying, an ex-fbi agent\'s guide to speed reading people. (1st ed.). New York, NY: Harper Paperbacks.
2 Ekman, P. (2008). Emotions revealed, recognizing faces and feelings to improve communication and emotional life. New York, NY: Owl Books.
3 Nierenberg, G., & Calero, H. (1971). How to read a person like a book. New York, NY: Pocket Books.
4 Ekman, P. (2009). Telling lies. New York, NY: W. W. Norton.
5 Navarro, J., & Schafer, J. (2001). Detecting deception. FBI Law Enforcement Bulletin, 9-12.
6 Hartley, G., & Karinch, M. (2005). How to spot a liar. Pompton Plains, NJ: The Career Press.
7 Ekman, P., & Friesen, W. (1974). Detecting deception from the body or face. Journal of Personality and Social

Psychology, 29, 288-298. doi: 10.1037/h0036006
8 Ekman, P., Friesen, W., & O'Sullivan, M. (1988). Smiles when lying. Journal of Personality and Social Psychology, 54, 414-420. doi: 10.1037/0022-3514.54.3.414
9 Ekman, P., & O'Sullivan, M. (1991). Who can catch a liar?. American Psychologist, 46(9), 913-920. doi: 10.1037/0003-066X.46.9.913
10 Ekman, P., O'Sullivan, M., & Frank, M. (1999). A few can catch a liar. Psychological Science, 10(3), 263-266. doi: 10.1111/1467-9280.00147
11 DePaulo, B., Stone, J., & Lassiter, G. (1985). Deceiving and detecting deceit. In B. Schlenker (Ed.), The self and social life (pp. 323-370). New York, NY: McGraw-Hill.
12 DePaulo, B., Lindsay, J., Malone, B., Muhlenbruck, L., Charlton, K., & Cooper, H. (2003). Cues to deception. Psychological Bulletin, 129, 74-112. doi: 10.1037/0033-2909.129.1.74
13 Ekman, P., Friesen, W., & Tomkins, S. (1971). Facial Affect Scoring Technique: A first validity study. Semiotica, 3(1), 37-58. doi: 10.1515/semi.1971.3.1.37
14 Ekman, P., & Friesen, W. (1984). Unmasking the face. (2 ed.). Palo Alto, CA: Consulting Psychologists Press.
15 Ekman, P., & Rosenberg, E. (2005). What the face reveals: Basic and applied studies of spontaneous expression using the facial action coding system (facs). (2 ed.). New York, NY: Oxford University Press.

Chapter Six: Signs of Deception

1 Navarro, J., & Schafer, J. (2001). Detecting deception.

References

FBI Law Enforcement Bulletin, 9-12.

2 Hartley, G., & Karinch, M. (2005). How to spot a liar. Pompton Plains, NJ: The Career Press.

3 Ekman, P. (2008). Emotions revealed, recognizing faces and feelings to improve communication and emotional life. New York, NY: Owl Books.

4 Navarro, J., & Karlins, M. (2008). What every body is saying, an ex-fbi agent\'s guide to speed reading people. (1st ed.). New York, NY: Harper Paperbacks.

5 Frank, M., Menasco, M., & O'Sullivan, M. (2008). Human behavior and deception detection. In J. Voeller (Ed.), Handbook of Science and Technology for Homeland Security (pp. 1-13). John Wiley & Sons, Inc. doi: 10.1002/9780470087923.hhs299

6 Ekman, P., Friesen, W., & O'Sullivan, M. (1988). Smiles when lying. Journal of Personality and Social Psychology, 54, 414-420. doi: 10.1037/0022-3514.54.3.414

7 Ekman, P., & Friesen, W. (1974). Detecting deception from the body or face. Journal of Personality and Social Psychology, 29, 288-298. doi: 10.1037/h0036006

8 Meyer, P. (2010). Liespotting. New York, NY: St. Martin's Press.

9 Nierenberg, G., & Calero, H. (1971). How to read a person like a book. New York, NY: Pocket Books.

10 Ekman, P., & Friesen, W. (1984). Unmasking the face. (2 ed.). Palo Alto, CA: Consulting Psychologists Press.

11 Ekman, P. (2009). Telling lies. New York, NY: W. W. Norton.

12 DePaulo, B., Lindsay, J., Malone, B., Muhlenbruck, L., Charlton, K., & Cooper, H. (2003). Cues to deception.

Psychological Bulletin, 129, 74-112. doi: 10.1037/0033-2909.129.1.74

13 Vrij, A., Edward, K., & Bull, R. (2001). Police officers' ability to detect deceit: The benefit of indirect deception detection measures. Legal Criminological Psychology, 6, 185-196. doi: 10.1348/135532501168271

14 Zuckerman, M., DePaulo, B., & Rosenthal, R. (1981). Verbal and nonverbal communication of deception. In L. Berkowitz (Ed.), Advances in Experimental Psychology (pp. 1-59). San Diego, CA: Academic Press. doi: 10.1016/S0065-2601(08)60369-X

15 Zuckerman, M., & Driver, R. (1985). Telling lies: Verbal and nonverbal correlates of deception. In A. Siegman & S. Feldstein (Eds.), Multichannel integration of nonverbal behavior (pp. 129-147). Hillsdale, NJ: Erlbaum.

16 Vrij, A., Edward, K., & Bull, R. (2001). Police officers' ability to detect deceit: The benefit of indirect deception detection measures. Legal Criminological Psychology, 6, 185-196. doi: 10.1348/135532501168271

17 Mann, S., Vrij, A., & Bull, R. (2004). Detecting true lies: Police officers' abilities to detect suspects' lies. Journal of Applied Psychology, 89, 137-149. doi: 10.1037/0021-9010.89.1.137

18 Hess, U., & Kleck, R. (1990). Differentiating emotion elicited and deliberate emotional facial expressions. European Journal of Social Psychology, 20, 369-385. doi: 10.1002/ejsp.2420200502

19 Hess, U., & Kleck, R. (1994). The cues decoders use in attempting to differentiate emotion-elicited and posed facial expressions. European Journal of Social Psychology,

References

24, 367-381. doi: 10.1002/ejsp.2420240306

20 Schmidt, K., Bhattacharya, S., & Denlinger, R. (2009). Comparison of deliberate and spontaneous facial movement in smiles and eyebrow raises. Journal of Nonverbal Behavior, 33, 35-45. doi: 10.1007/s10919-008-0058-6

21 Ekman, P., Hager, J., & Friesen, W. (1981). The symmetry of emotional and deliberate facial actions. The Society for Psychophysiological Research, 18(2), 101-106. doi: 10.1111/j.1469-8986.1981.tb02919.x

22 Hager, J., & Ekman, P. (1985). The asymmetry of facial actions is inconsistent with models of hemispheric specialization. Psychophysiology, 22(3), 307-318. doi: 10.1111/j.1469-8986.1985.tb01605.x

23 Ekman, P., Davidson, R., & Friesen, W. (1990). The Duchenne smile: Emotional expression and brain physiology II. Journal of Personality and Social Psychology, 58, 342-353. doi: 10.1037/0022-3514.58.2.342

24 Fox, N., & Davidson, R. (1987). Electroencephalogram asymmetry in response to the approach of a stranger and maternal separation in 10-month old children. Developmental Psychology, 23, 233-240. doi: 10.1037/0012-1649.23.2.233

25 Fox, N., & Davidson, R. (1988). Patterns on brain electrical activity during facial signs of emotion in 10-month old infants. Developmental Psychology, 24, 230-236. doi: 10.1037/0012-1649.24.2.230

• • •

A Guide To Deception

Index

Acknowledgements, 7

Action Unit, 54

Appendix, 71

Arms, 60, 73

Asymmetrical Expressions, 64

Auditory Stimuli, 27

B

Body Language, *See also* Micro-expressions, Nonverbal Behaviors, Signs of Deception

    Breathing, 62, 75

    Emotional Expression, 64

    Eyes, 58, 72

    Feet and Legs, 61, 74

    Hands and Arms, 60, 73

    Head and Neck, 59, 73

    Mouth, 59, 73

    Speech, 62, 75

Bond and DePaulo, 47

Bond and Robinson, 32

Breathing, 62, 75

Bull, 46

C

Cerebral Hemisphere, 65

Chapter Five, 51

Chapter Four, 43

Chapter One, 25

Index

Chapter Six, 57

Chapter Three, 37

Chapter Two, 29

Chimpanzee, 33

Cluster, 52, 68

Conclusion, 67

Contents, 9

D

Dedication, 5

Defining Deception, 29

Definition of Deception, 30, 32, 34, 35

    Ekman, 34

    Krauss, 30

    Mitchell, 32

    Vrij, 35

DeWaal, 33

Docan-Morgan, 46

Driskell, 45

E

Ekman, 34, 46

Ekman and Friesen, 54

Ekman and O'Sullivan, 43

Ekman, O'Sullivan, and Frank, 44

Emotional Expression, 64

- Asymmetrical, 64
- Non-spontaneous, 64
- Spontaneous, 64
- Symmetrical, 64

Eyes, 58, 72

F

Facial Action Coding System, 46, 54

FACS, 46, 54

Feet and Legs, 61, 74

Forward, 11

H

Index

Hands and Arms, 60, 73
Head and Neck, 59, 73
High-Steak Lie, 38
How To Use This Book, 19

I

Index, 89
Introduction, 17

K

Krauss, 30

L

Leakage, 49, 53
Legs, 61, 74
Lies, 37 *See also* Types of Lies
    Low-Steak, 37
    High-Steak, 38
List of Deceptive Behaviors, 71

Low-Steak Lie, 37

M

Meyer, 46

Micro-expressions *See also* Body Language, Nonverbal Behaviors, Signs of Deception

    Breathing, 62, 75

    Emotional Expression, 64

    Eyes, 58, 72

    Feet and Legs, 61, 74

    Hands and Arms, 60, 73

    Head and Neck, 59, 73

    Mouth, 59, 73

    Speech, 62, 75

Mitchell and Anderson, 33

Mitchell, 32

Monkey, 33

Mouth, 59, 73

N

Index

Navarro, 46

Neck, 59, 73

Nierenberg and Calero, 48

Non-spontaneous Expressions, 64

Nonverbal Behaviors, *See also* Body Language, Micro-expressions, Signs of Deception

> Breathing, 62, 75
>
> Emotional Expression, 64
>
> Eyes, 58, 72
>
> Feet and Legs, 61, 74
>
> Hands and Arms, 60, 73
>
> Head and Neck, 59, 73
>
> Mouth, 59, 73
>
> Speech, 62, 75

O'Sullivan, 47

Ophrys Speculum, 32

Orchid, 32

P

Porter, et al, 45

R

References, 77

S

Signs Of Deception, 57 *See also* Body Language, Micro-expressions Nonverbal Behaviors

    Breathing, 62, 75

    Emotional Expression, 64

    Eyes, 58, 72

    Feet and Legs, 61, 74

    Hands and Arms, 60, 73

    Head and Neck, 59, 73

    Mouth, 59, 73

    Speech, 62, 75

Speech, 62, 75

Speed of Light, 27

Speed of Sound, 27

Index

Spontaneous Expressions, 64

Symmetrical Expressions, 64

The Ability To Detect Deception, 43

The Body's Betrayal, 51

The Truth Hurts, 25, 28

Types of Lies, 37

    Low-Steak Lie, 37

    High-Steak Lie, 38

Visual Stimuli, 27

Vrij, 35, 45

W

Wasp, 32

What This Means For You, 67

Why The Truth Hurts, 25

A Guide To Deception

Why You Need This Book, 17
Wizards, 44, 47

A Guide To Deception

www.ingramcontent.com/pod-product-compliance
Lightning Source LLC
Chambersburg PA
CBHW071722040426
42446CB00011B/2179